THE
Archive Photographs
SERIES

SCARBOROUGH
IN THE '50S AND '60S

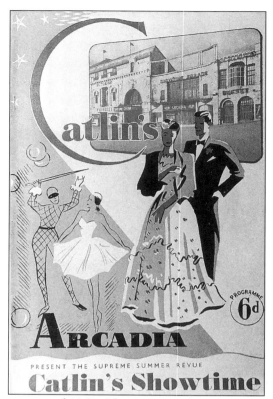

An Arcadia Programme cover of 1950. The first Arcadia was opened in 1903. Will Catlin bought it in 1909 and immediately demolished it and erected one of his own. The Arcadia Theatre seen on this photograph was originally the Palladium Picture House which had been built on the empty site between the then Arcadia Restaurant and the Arcadia Theatre. The Futurist Theatre now covers the site of the first Catlin's Arcadia Theatre.

THE
Archive Photographs
SERIES

SCARBOROUGH
IN THE '50S AND '60S

Compiled by
Richard James Percy

CHALFORD

First published 1994
Reprinted 1996
Copyright © Richard James Percy, 1994

The Chalford Publishing Company
St Mary's Mill, Chalford,
Stroud, Gloucestershire, GL6 8NX

ISBN 0 7524 0007 X

Typesetting and origination by
The Chalford Publishing Company
Printed in Great Britain by
Redwood Books, Trowbridge

The Spa Chalet at the southern end of the Cliff Bridge was built in 1859 by the Cliff Bridge Company for the General Manager of the Spa, George Reeves Smith. It has changed little over the years. The same cannot be said of the bridge which was opened in 1827. The ornate gates and toll booths were taken down the year after the tolls were abolished in 1951.

Contents

Introduction   6

1.   The 1950s   9

2.   The 1960s   83

Acknowledgements   160

Introduction

Scarborough had emerged from the Second World War in 1945 slightly battle-scarred but eager to regain her position as one of the east coast's top resorts.

This was not as simple as it looked. There were over three thousand homeless people on the housing list and they took priority over any ambitious scheme for the town. The only solution lay in housing estates. Work had started on the Sandybed and Barrowcliff estates in 1945 using prisoners of war. By 1950 Barrowcliff alone boasted nine hundred and sixty houses. Naturally, such a large community required a public house, and after the Health and Housing Committee considered the plans forwarded to them by Scarborough architects Alderson and Allen, who were acting on behalf of Samuel Smith, Tadcaster Brewers, they recommended to the town council that such a building be built.

When talks were in progress about the future development of Scarborough in 1946 it was decided that Eastfield was the best site for an estate. Work had started on what today is a huge estate resembling a small town in April, 1949, but, by March, 1950, only ten houses had been built owing to the lack of bricklayers in Scarborough. It was hoped to accommodate ten thousand people on the estate by 1970. Today's figure far outnumbers the original calculations and Eastfield now boasts public houses, churches, schools and a library. If ever an estate can be called a success then Eastfield must surely rank near the top.

Unemployment has always been a problem in Scarborough and what vacancies did, and to a certain degree still do, occur are usually of a seasonal nature. During the 1950s and 1960s this problem was more acute because of the fact that the town had no industry whatsoever on its outskirts, whereas today, even though there is an unemployment problem, the town for its size has a fair proportion of industry.

In January, 1950, there were eight hundred and seventeen men and three hundred and eleven women seeking work. The dole was 26/- (£1.30) per week, but it was hoped that as the season got into full swing, and by this time Scarborough was once again the premier resort on the east coast, this number would decrease with the many vacancies opening up in the hotels and cafés.

It had been a hard, uphill struggle in the five years since the cessation of hostilities for Scarborough to achieve and regain her status. The visitors had been willing to come on holiday and, to be fair, many did, but not in the numbers required to make a town prosper. The trouble had lain in the lack of accommodation. To be truthful, there simply wasn't any. All the hotels and boarding houses were still in the hands of the military as were many places of entertainment including the Spa and the Floral Hall. Thousands of troops were billeted in these buildings and it was well into 1947 before they were de-requisitioned. Even then the problem was not solved overnight. There were shortages of soap and linen and many of the hotels had given their furniture to the Americans to furnish their billets. All this plus the added discomfort of the frequent power cuts due to the electricity supply not working to full capacity hardly encouraged a flow of holidaymakers. But all was overcome in time and Scarborough settled down to enjoy the profits from its seasonal visitors.

To be absolutely honest, the 1950s for Scarborough marked the end of her reign as Queen of the Yorkshire Coast. She was not unique; it was a national trend as families flew off to sample the delights of foreign resorts.

For those who do not remember Scarborough's heyday, and only know the town as it is today, it must be very difficult to imagine the beauty of the well-kept gardens and parks, where no hint of vandalism was to be seen. The streets, before demolition robbed the town of architecturally interesting buildings such as the Pavilion and the Balmoral Hotels, Bar Church and Rowntrees Department Store, were a delight to walk down, with interesting shops, long before the days of the supermarket, which stocked a wide variety of goods.

Scarborough had a quaint, Victorian atmosphere, and the stroll along the seafront, with none of the traffic problems of today, only the clatter of horses' hooves as the cabs plied their trade back and forth, made it the ideal setting for young families. There were the icecream parlours, souvenir shops, just three amusement arcades, donkey rides, the Punch and Judy man, the pebble stalls and Gala Land.

Gala Land, that vast underground delight, smelling so musty, yet unique and appealing, could accommodate over a thousand people and had every attraction from the dodgems to a theatre. It was demolished in the late 1960s and replaced by a white elephant of an underground car park.

As the 1950s rolled on people's tastes changed, as indeed did the holidaymakers themselves. Whereas at one time families would have booked into an hotel or boarding house for a week's stay, the norm was now for day trippers to arrive by the thousands on the many excursion trains that had been laid on for them. They would make their way down to the beach and remain there till it was time to depart. It was a bonanza for the seafront traders but hardly encouraging for the hoteliers and boarding house keepers.

Shrewd businessmen noticed this new trend and exploited it to the full. One such man who helped change the face of Scarborough's seafront was Albert Corrigan, who had been born in a caravan at Holbeck Moor near Leeds in 1904 into what was and still is a well-known showbiz family.

He and his brother had settled in Scarborough in 1947 and opened up two amusement arcades. Mr. Corrigan felt that now was the time was ripe to speculate, and in the mid-1950s introduced bingo to the resort. The people loved it and over the next few years a string of bingo arcades stretching the length of the seafront vied for the many customers who flocked down to play the game.

As the bingo fad faded somewhat Mr. Corrigan again speculated and was responsible for the first Wimpy Bar in town, which was situated at the corner of Northway.

By the late 1950s Scarborough Council was concentrating on what was its main policy, that of changing the face of the town and creating a super modern resort but at the same time hoping to retain its Victorian elegance. Whole streets were demolished and in their place modern flats and houses were built. Whether or not the council achieved its objective is rather debatable, and most Scarborians have very definite views.

Private enterprise on the other hand seemed to triumph somewhat better, and the Zoo and Marineland were successful and introduced to the town something new and exciting. Other ambitious plans, such as trams along the Marine Drive and a mono-rail, never did come to fruition.

One success organized by the town council was the Dutch Festival. This was first held in 1957 and it drew in unprecedented crowds, especially to watch the Grand Procession which was the highlight of the week's attractions. Over the years the name has changed. Be it the Benelux Festival or the Scarborough Fayre, the programme remains the same.

Even so, the powers-that-be still seemed to be floundering in a morass of indecision over the future of the town. It was obviously not working trying to run a town on both Victorian and modern principals. It either had to be one or the other. The events of the 1960s would solve the problem for good.

Youth suddenly sprung up, rebellious and craving excitement. There was no violence – in fact compared with today it was all very tame – but at the time it was looked on as being a minor revolution.

Until the mid-1960s Scarborough had no nightclubs of any importance; the only entertainment being the Spa, the Olympia, the many church hall dances and the picture houses – the Odeon, Capital, Aberdeen, Londesborough and Futurist. When coffee bars were introduced to the town with their juke boxes these places became the 'in' spots to be; all rather monastical by today's standards but things were changing and quickly.

Almost overnight local pop groups were formed, influenced by the Beatles and the Mersey Sound. Suddenly Scarborough was in the twentieth century whether she liked it or not. Nightclubs were granted permission to open and by 1966/67 such placed as Hairy Bobs Cavern, 2Bs, Michaels, and the Candlelight were considered 'in' places. The Futurist Cinema was converted into a theatre, and top names such as the Beatles, the Rolling Stones, the Kinks and Roy Orbison played there to screaming fans.

Scarborough's bands were suddenly in great demand and names such as the Moonshots, the Mandrakes, Strawboa Fantasy, Electraz, Chows Men and the Panthers were known throughout the district and further afield, often supporting the top names in the world of pop. By the end of the decade Scarborough was being hailed as the 'pop centre' of the north.

They were heady days, vibrant and exciting. New shops opened up catering exclusively for the younger generation; a trend unheard of until them. There was Surfing Scene, Messengers Boutique and Carnaby Street, all stocked with the latest gear – hipsters, tank tops and reefer jackets.

As the '60s ended and the '70s took over violence was beginning to show its ugly head. Scarborough became the centre for the gangs of mods who arrived in their hundreds on their scooters. What had once been Brighton's problem suddenly became very local. Tempers flared, resulting in the mods blaming the police for harassment and vice versa. Luckily, as with most trends, the invasion of the mods faded into insignificance and today it is a thing of the past.

It had taken a mere twenty five years since the end of the war for Scarborough to lose her identity; a transition from the Victorian to the modern that was not applauded in all quarters. Gone forever was the relaxed way of life that had once been Scarborough. What was sown in those infant days of the 1960s is being reaped today. Lying derelict are many of the town's former attractions simply because people's tastes no longer permit them to enjoy, for example, outdoor concerts at the Open Air Theatre or swimming in the South Bay Pool. Today the majority of visitors are young people who crave night life and pubs, leaving only a small percentage of the holidaymakers to enjoy what remains of the town's attractions.

The green belt is no more and vast industrial estates encircle the town; what were once outlying villages are now joined and resemble suburbs of Scarborough.

Policies and progress have made the town what it is today and it will be the prerogative of future historians to judge the rights and wrongs of the changes.

One
The 1950s

On Tuesday, 20th December, 1949 a Christmas Party was held at the Boys' Club, North Street to welcome in the coming year. Seen joining in the singing is Mr. H. Whitehead, President of the Scarborough Rotary, who is standing next to Mr. Ernie Jaconelli and his accordion.

It's take your partners for the Veleta as Constance and Ernest Leather lead off on the floor of the Olympia Ballroom in 1950. For any lady interested the dress was in cream lace over brown satin.

On 12th May, 1950 every school in Scarborough received ten 40lb boxes of apples as a gift from the peoples of the Empire. These apples had been distributed from the Commonwealth Gift Centre, London and had been sent to the U.K. by Mr. A.K. Lloyd, President of the British Columbia Tree Fruits Ltd., acting on behalf of the growers. Here we see the pupils of Northstead School receiving their apples. On the left, with mistress Mrs. Lee, can be seen Margaret Messruther, Bunty Leather, Trevor Bailey and Ann Crawford. The mistress on the right is Miss Scott.

Work started on the erection of prefabricated buildings at Sandybed in July, 1945. Tarrans of Hull were the building contractors and German prisoners of war were brought in to lay the roads. This view taken from Red House in 1950 shows a completely different estate from the one of today. Many of the properties are now privately owned and, with the many flowering shrubs and trees, Sandybed has become a prime residential area.

It was on 1st June, 1950 that the *Hispaniola*, not to be confused with the boat on the Mere, the last of the Great British sailing ships, anchored in the harbour after its long journey from Appledore. She had been launched at Glasson Dock, Lancaster in 1887 under the name of *Ryelands*. She had carried grain until 1948. Here we see the Mayor and Mayoress (Councillor and Mrs. Chapman) greeting the skipper, Lieut-Commander S. Gorrell, on board the boat which was converted into an aquarium.

The Scalby 2nd eleven Cricket Team in 1951. Front row, left to right: Charlie Nendick, Brian Kettlewell. Middle row: Brian Lewis, Johnny Foster, Dick Barkham (Captain), Dennis Bielby, Ernie Sedman. Back row: Mr. Butterwick (Umpire), Walter Brown, Bill Temple, Jeff Walker, Ray Bastiman.

Here we see the grand old lady herself, the *Hispaniola*, moored to the pier in 1951. Hundreds of holidaymakers visited the Hispanioquarium as it became known. One couple, Mr. and Mrs. S.L. Lawrence of Leeds, purchased the 100,000th ticket and were rewarded by being given free admission to all the town's attractions. In 1954 the old ship was taken to Hull, where she became a museum until she appeared in the film *Moby Dick* and was wrecked, a sad end to an old lady of the sea.

On 20th May, 1951 over eight hundred members of the British Red Cross Society met at Burniston Barracks, where the Princess Royal, Commander-in-Chief of the Society, presented new colours to the branch. The only faces known on this group are, from the left, 7th Louie Orr, 11th Flora Watson and 13th Ellen Berry. The barracks are, at the time of writing, being demolished.

Mayor's Day, 1951. Tables are seen set out in civic splendour in the Royal Hotel's Ballroom and Meeting Room for the new Mayor, Alderman J.W. Hardcastle.

The St. Thomas Street of 1951 and the street of today are hardly recognisable as being the same. Only a few of the original buildings remain, the rest being demolished in 1957. Seen on this photograph are, left to right: Dawnya Pickering, Christine Brown (wearing what the other girls called her 'Alice Blue Gown'), Bunty Leather and Mrs. Constance Leather.

Two ladies from the chorus of the Scarborough Amateur Operatic Society's 1952 production of the *Desert Song* pose with two stage-struck donkeys, Jesse and Peggy.

Hardwick's Bus Service ran from 56 Victoria Road until well into the 1970s, when their depot was demolished and Postgate House Flats built on the site. This photograph taken in 1951 shows one of the buses that ran to Forge Valley, Ayton and Ebberston.

This splendid view taken from the Cliff Bridge in 1951 captures the fine sweep of the South Bay with the impressive Spa, the Clock Tower Cafe and, fading into the distance below the elegant Esplanade, the South Bay Pool. Just visible on the horizon is the Holbeck Hall Hotel, which in June, 1993 crashed into the sea. It had originally been called Wheatcliffe, the home of George A. Smith, becoming an hotel in about 1932 when it was bought by the Laughton family.

In the 1950s and '60s, when Scarborough's Railway Station, especially during the summer months, had a train arriving every few minutes, the hoards of holidaymakers needed somewhere to quench their thirst. The B.R. Refreshment Rooms were open until 12 every night, seven days a week, and needed a large staff. The rooms above the refreshment rooms, which at one time had been the Railway Hotel, were used as staff bedrooms. Photographed in 1952, a number of the staff pose in the forecourt. Left to right: Louie Orr, Miss Alcock (Manageress), Clara Cooper (Assistant Manageress), Dorothy Leppington, Ethel Messheader, Bennita Scarborough, Mrs. Golder and Ida Gibson.

Scarborough's fish pier in the 1950s and '60s was a hive of industry, keeping many fishing families in work. Jack Morris, from one of them, is seen centre holding the basket. He little knew that in years to come foreign laws issuing forth from Europe would damage Great Britain's fishing industry and govern the lives of the fishing community at large.

A peaceful day in November, 1952 is only broken by the road drill as Ramshill Road is widened. The house on the left which had been converted into a Post Office and bank was originally called Mount Devon Lodge and was a private school. The ground floor of the house on the right is now greatly altered.

It was a wet, dismal day on Friday, 8th February, 1952 when the Mayor (Councillor J.W. Hardcastle) stood on the dais in the Town Hall gardens surrounded by robed members of the council to read the proclamation declaring Elizabeth Queen of Great Britain and the Commonwealth and of her other territories overseas. One or two cameramen have taken advantage of the Royal Hotel's balcony to get a better view.

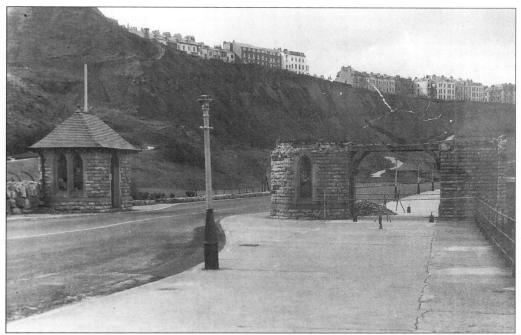

In April, 1953 the North Toll House on the Marine Drive was demolished. In January of that year the Water and Streets Committee had had numerous requests from traders who wished to turn the booths into shops. Only one member of the council, Nathan Walsh, was for this; the others thought the Toll House caused a dangerous bottle-neck for traffic.

Sir Thomas Dugdale, Minister of Agriculture, is seen welcoming Mr. Winston Churchill as he steps out of his car on the Spa where he was attending the 1952 Conservative Conference.

Mrs. Churchill in silver/gold top and pearls is introduced by the town's Mayor (Councillor J.W. Hardcastle) to civic heads as they enter the ballroom of the (presumably) Grant Hotel, where she and her husband were staying whilst in town to attend the Conservative Conference.

The two waitresses and the Mayor seem a little concerned over Mrs. Churchill's delicate handling of the bread roll, or could it be that they are completely overawed by her presence? Whatever the reason, Mrs. Churchill is oblivious to all and calmly enjoys her meal.

On 31st January, 1953 the east coast of Britain was subjected to violent storms that resulted in the deaths of two hundred and ninety people. In Scarborough the storm broke shortly after tea. Six foot high waves rushed across the Foreshore, ripping up railings and roadway. Cars overturned and seafront property was damaged. Throughout the town the storm took its toll. T.V. aerials, chimneys and trees were blown down, and over six hundred council houses alone suffered damage.

On the North Side there was extensive damage, and on this photograph one can see the wreckage from over one hundred beach chalets that simply broke up like matchwood as the mighty waves smashed into them. At the height of the storm hundreds of frightened rats swarmed out of the sewers and ran across the road.

Clearing up operations began in earnest after the storm. Workmen are seen here outside the Olympia Ballroom and Cafe. Notice Pacitto's windows boarded up after iron railings had been hurled through them by the force of the water.

The morning after the storm, and the Spa looks as if a bomb has exploded.

The next period when the seafront would be subjected to high tides was on 12th February, 1953. After their experience the traders took precautions, and here we see workmen laying sandbags outside Evelyn's Cafe under the Grand Hotel. Luckily there was no repetition of January.

The Mayor (Councillor J.W. Hardcastle), seen on the right, discusses the damage caused by the storm. The entrance to the Olympia Ballroom is seen on the far right.

The *Avago*, an ex-R.A.F. target launch which had been privately bought by a man who hoped to turn it into a houseboat but had been refused permission over sanitary arrangements, was swept out of the harbour, across the bay, and ended up smashed against the sea wall near Children's Corner. The next day all that remained was a piece of wood.

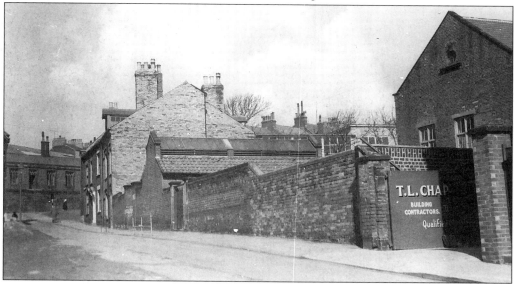

Taken in 1953, this view of Auborough Street looking up to Castle Road shows St. Peter's School, which closed in 1993, on the right. The house at the top right was demolished a couple of years after this photograph was taken. Running across the top can be seen Wilson's Mariners Asylum. These almshouses were built by Richard Wilson in 1836 for the use of 'decayed mariners'. The architect was John Barry. They were renovated in 1922.

Tuesday, 2nd June, 1953 was Coronation Day, and throughout the town parties were held (indoors due to the bad weather) to celebrate the occasion. Here we see the partygoers of Tindall Street standing in the doorway of Gladstone Road Chapel. Front row, left to right: Graham Cracknell (who seems to be having trouble with his hat), Pete Eade, Steve Moore and Avril Stevens. Second row: Wendy Bartle, Geoff Boyes, Gwen Rowden and Ann Eade. Third row: Christine Scaife (holding Barbara Payne), John Collishaw, Dave Moore, Richard Collishaw and Fred Eade.

Fireworks and rockets burst over the ancient Castle Keep, creating a dazzling finale to the Coronation Day celebrations.

Hinderwell County Modern School infants, 1953. Left to right: Pauline Rumford, Billy Keen, Christine Millington, Richard Percy, Steven Davison, Jennifer Walker, Irene Agar, Angela Gooch, Rosie Hodds and Joe Bamfield.

The building facing centre is the old Cattle Tavern in Hope Street, so named from the slaughterhouses that stood near. It dated back to 1852, when it was opened as a beerhouse, and remained so until 1904, when it lost its license due to the pressure from the local clergy who protested about the number of licensed premises in town. The old building was finally demolished in the late 1950s.

Seen keeping in touch with home by reading the *Scarborough Mercury* is 20 year old sergeant Marmaduke Vickerman. At the time of this photograph in 1953 he had already served three years of a five year stint in the terrorist-infested British colony of Malaya. Sergeant Vickerman, who was stationed at Ipoh in the State of Perak, served in the intelligence section of the combined police and military operations room.

Johnson's fish restaurant staff, Sandside, 1953. Today it is an amusement arcade. The only faces known are, from the left: 2nd Mrs. Fishburn, 5th Lorna Cooper, 7th Miss Johnson (whose father was the owner) and Mrs. Annie Edmonds.

During the first week of the booking office being opened over seventy thousand people had booked seats for the Scarborough Amateur Operatic Society's 1953 production of *Annie Get Your Gun*, which, like all the society's shows, was held at the Open Air Theatre. Seen here are the gentlemen of the chorus: A. Webb, D. Trott, J. Pobgee, K. Pack, F. Mellor, L. Mason, W. Kidd, N. Jewison, J. Hudson, M. Crosier, A. Crawford, W. Blackburn, F. Bell and J. Boag.

On Saturday, 18th July, 1953 the Mayor (Councillor N. Walsh) was welcomed aboard the cruiser H.M.S. *Swiftsure* by the Captain, T.L. Bratt. At night the *Swiftsure* gave a firework display. The ship, weighing 8,000 tons, was launched in 1943 and completed the following year.

The Sun Inn on the left is still there, but that is the only clue for those who do not remember St. Thomas Street as it was when this photograph was taken in 1954. The space on the left is where the Theatre Royal had stood. It had been built in the 1730s and was demolished in 1924.

Here we see another view of St. Thomas Street, taken from St. Nicholas Street in 1954, three years before the property on the right was demolished. The building on the left was built about 1790 and was a noted Coffee House. In 1811 it was opened by John Cole as a library. Over the years the premises have been used by Mr. Storry, tea dealer; Bevan Harris, draper; J. Smith, watchmaker; Mr. Webb, tailor; Mr. Thompson, draper, and Greensmith and Thackwray, hosiers.

Annie Get Your Gun at the Open Air Theatre in 1953 had a chorus of two hundred and a ballet of twenty five. Here we see two of the principals striking an artistic pose. Left to right: William Thomson as Col. W.F. Cody and Edwin Smith as Pawnee Bill.

The fastest gun in the West? Well, maybe not, but Ann Doonan looks the perfect Annie Oakley (except for the red nail varnish!), playing opposite the other lead, Glen Martin, in *Annie Get Your Gun*.

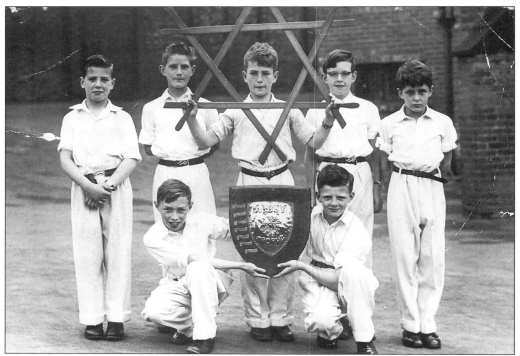

St. Martins-on-the-Hill Junior School's sword dancing team toured the district giving displays. They won the Abbey Trophy three years in succession. This photograph, taken about 1954, shows the team; the only boys known are Geoff Pearson, John Green, Robert Cromack and Robert Wilde.

Martin Lawrence took the title role in the Scarborough Amateur Operatic Society's 1954 production of *Chu Chin Chow*. Here he stands in regal splendour surrounded by the ladies and gentlemen of the chorus.

The Crackers Concert Party was formed in 1946 by Lesley Sturdy. Their 'home' was the Arcadia Theatre, where the cast are seen posing in 1954. Back row, left to right: Billy Proctor, Joan Billington, Alan Aldred, Wilf Eccles, Valerie Neil, Derrick Trott, Gladys Maughan, Tom Hughes and Fred Cooper. Middle row: Brian Shannon, David Stephenson, Mildred King, Joan Reedie, Jim Maughan, Doris Waller, Lesley Sturdy, Doris Hudson, Mrs. Laycock, Ernest Reed and James Waller. Front row: Dennis York, Dorothy Wilkinson, Edith Reedie, Cissie Webster, Norman Waite, Marie Cooper, Mrs. A. Sturdy, Sheila Rhynehart, Harold Cutts, Billy Webster, Connie Eccles and Marjorie Taylor.

On Monday, 31st May, 1954 Councillor and Mrs. Miles Bird were elected Mayor and Mayoress of Scarborough. The Mayor's motto for the year was, 'Forward'. Here we see Mrs. Bird being decorated with her Chain of Office.

A 'glittering show' was how the adverts described the local amateur production of *Chu Chin Chow* in 1954. Martin Lawrence sits like a benevolent potentate surrounded by his courtiers. Left to right: Nut Al-Huda-Aki (Harry Hapgood), Mayjannah (Ellen De Toit), Mahbubah (Wynna Evans), Ali Baba (George Noon), Al-Kulub (Wendy Elliot), Baba Mustafa (Norman Carr), Alcolom (Margaret Kilby), Kasim (Shaun Glenville) and Abdullah (Edwin Smith).

Ladies of the chorus of *Chu Chin Chow* included Nell Berry, Marion Asprey, Una Johnson, Margaret Boag and Mary King.

The Social Club members of E.T.W. Dennis & Sons Ltd. held their supper dance at the Palm Court Hotel on Friday, 12th November, 1954. Seen on the photograph are Flo Spivey, Anne Stephenson, Frances Ward, Betty Joyce, Mr. Webb, Lily Wilson, Joan Skelton, Wilf Drybold, Cicerly Webb, Mr. and Mrs. Howe, June Bowtell, Ray Marsden, Enid Sedman and Murial Longhorn. Seated on the second row are Arnold, Herbert, Jeffrey and Stephen Dennis.

In 1951 Mr. Herbert Powers and Mrs. Margaret Moore established a business in a small shop at 83 Victoria Road. They called it the Office Equipment Bureau. The property is now demolished. This photograph taken in 1954 shows Mr. F. Moore (with moustache) and Mr. Powers in the doorway of the shop. The business flourished and they moved to premises opposite and later to their present site in Victoria Road.

Auborough House at the top of Auborough Street was said to be the most interesting house in Scarborough. For years it had been the home of the brewery family, Nesfield. In 1913 it was bequeathed to the vicar of the Parish Church for use as a vicarage. Because the church failed to fulfil the conditions it was sold in 1914 to Councillor White for £420. By 1953 it lay derelict and was demolished shortly afterwards. St. Mary's Parish House now stands on the site.

Boarded up windows on the houses at the corner of Auborough Street and Friarsway in 1955 are a sure sign that demolition is soon to take place. The shop on the corner, 2 Auborough Street, belonged to Harold Longhorn, boot repairer, until the war. At the time of this photograph Mrs. Scott had only just vacated the premises. Between 2 and 4 Auborough Street ran a passageway that led into Moorhouse's Yard. Today the widened street covers the site.

Keith Corrie began playing the piano accordion at the age of eight. He went on to play with Max Jaffa at the Spa and on the Hughie Green Show at the Floral Hall. Keith was one of the first members to join the Y.M.C.A. Review Group when it was formed in 1964. In 1967 he was awarded the Jimmy Savile Trophy for being best all-rounder in the club.

King Richard III House, Sandside has delighted both young and old over the years. The king is reputed to have lodged at the house when he was Lord High Admiral to his brother Edward IV in 1484. In 1914 a Manchester antique dealer opened up the place as a museum with Mr. E.H. Burrows who hailed from Birmingham as the manager. The owner was drowned on the *Lusitania* and Mr. Burrows took over. The house remained in the family until 1964, when it became a café.

The Grand Hotel staff in 1955. Back row, left to right: William Blackburn, -?-, Mr. Wardman, -?-, Tony Emmett and George Edmonds. Front row: the Assistant Manager, -?-, Bernard Stead, -?-, Louis Roberts (Head Chef, who at one time worked at the Pavilion Hotel), -?-, Joe Young (Pattiserie), George Picton and Mr. Robinson (store keeper).

The magnificent Spa Grand Hall designed by Verity and Hunt was opened in 1879 having been built on the burnt-out remains of Sir Joseph Paxton's Grand Hall of 1857. Over the years the top names in the world of entertainment have appeared there. Seen here appearing for the beginning of the 1955 season is Charles Shadwell and his Orchestra. Admission was 1/- (5p), weekly tickets 17/6d (87p) or a seasonal ticket cost £3.10s (£3.50).

George Edmonds stands at the doorway of Henry Johnson's Fish Restaurant, Sandside, where he worked as a fish frier in the early 1950s. Today the whole building has been turned into an amusement arcade.

This view shows Longwestgate looking towards Friarsway in 1955. The pathway on the left led up to Ebenezer Place which got its name from the Ebenezer Chapel which stood behind the wall. The chapel was build in 1827 and restored in 1856. It closed in the 1940s and became the Sports Arena until 1952, when a fire broke out in an upstairs room. Fire engines rushed to the scene and neighbouring property was evacuated. All that remained the following morning was a burnt-out shell which was later demolished. Today flats stand on the site.

These girls enjoying a day on the sands in the mid-1950s worked at Firth & Wilsons, Vernon Road. Left to right: Rita Cammish, Edie Buckle, Madge Rowe, Dulcie Raper, Dot Eves, Alma Wharton (Dulcie's sister), Doreen Redfern, Doris Beadle, Marie Jacques and Joan Taylor.

Ladies and gentlemen of the chorus of the 1955 production of *Oklahoma* pose on the stage of the Open Air Theatre.

Work started on the demolition of St. Thomas Street in early 1955. One of the first buildings to go was the Food Office, the empty space on the photograph. This office had formally belonged to Pindar's the Printers. Opposite can be seen Broadbent's carpet shop. This block came down a year or two later and Victoria's Nightclub was built on the site.

It is not very often that photographers capture the backs of properties on film but here we see what is recorded as being the back yards of the houses in North Terrace. This may not be correct as a later photograph showing the front of North Terrace looks totally different if one compares the chimneys.

On one summer evening in 1955 eight thousand spectators – a full house – watched the Scarborough Amateur Operatic Society's production of Oklahoma at the Open Air Theatre. These shows were considered Scarborough's main attraction and, whatever the weather, nothing seemed to dampen people's enthusiasm for the shows.

With its natural backcloth of trees and the shimmering lake at the foot of the stage, the Open Air Theatre had a fairly tale atmosphere. It was the Lord Mayor of London who said when opening the theatre in 1932, 'I doubt whether anything of this kind has ever previously been seen in England.' This particular view shows the finale of *Oklahoma*.

The houses may look a little dilapidated, but what character and what possibilities they offered to a council who had already condemned them when this photograph was taken in 1955. It is of course Auborough Street looking up towards the Scarborough Arms pub. Today the widened road covers the site.

Here we see another view of Auborough Street in 1955. The fish shop is still there today and is the only clue as to where the view is for those too young to remember the street as it was.

On 14th April, 1955 H.R.H. Princess Alexandra, dressed in a deep red coat and matching frock, arrived in town to receive purses for the National Union of Teachers' Benevolent and Orphans' Fund. She is seen here meeting members of the crew of the lifeboat and the relations of the men who had died in the December tragedy when the lifeboat overturned. Left to right: the Mayor (Councillor Miles Bird), Denk Mainprize (Coxswain), Bill Sheader (behind H.R.H.), Tom Rowley, Alan Rennard, Colin Jenkinson, Fred Normandale and Jacky Readman.

Parked in the snow outside the Wessex Hotel on the Esplanade in January, 1956 is the Office Equipment van. The driver would be visiting the hotels and servicing their typewriters.

It's Aggie's Boxing Day birthday outing at the Golden Last pub, Eastborough in 1956. Left to right: Aggie Dunkerton, Joyce Phillips, Ted Dunkerton, 'Uncle Dunk', Bill Phillips, Paul Dunkerton and Joe Griffiths. The Golden Last dates back to the 1700s, although there has been much renovation over the years and it is very difficult to find any trace of the original building. What one sees today possibly dates from 1856 when Eastborough was constructed.

This neat terrace of houses is St. Thomas's Walk. When this photograph was taken in 1956 the houses were already over one hundred years old. At one time the rents had been 5/- (25p) per week which had to be paid into the Rates Office. It was a street of characters. Mr. Watson who sold milk from cans hanging on a yoke was nicknamed 'Old Cow Dick', and Isaac Bland ('Cockles and mussels alive-O') went under the endearing name of 'Pratty Gott'. A car park now covers the site.

Staff at Stockdales Potato Merchants, Knapton in 1956. A blue and cream coloured double decker bus picked up the workers at the Railway Station and drove them to the packing depot. Seen on the photograph from top to bottom are: Miss Beadham, Mervin Pearson, Pam Hardwicke, George Wilkie, Peggy Brearley, the two Mrs. Pearsons, Mary Furnish, Bob Crawford, Annie Cutts, John Westwood, Andrew Pearson and Charlie Whittaker.

King's Rhapsody, staged by the Scarborough Amateur Operatic Society in 1956, was described as a 'glittering extravaganza'. The costumes alone had cost £2,000. The costumes for the ballet dancers had been run up by the Wardrobe Mistress, Cis Appleby. The show had a cast of two hundred, a ballet of thirty and a number of West End principals. Left to right: Tom Gillis, Sheila Holt, Maxwell Deas, Jean Grayston (Max Jaffa's wife), Ann Trevor, Margaret Boag, Elaine Garreau, Mamie Benson, Edwin Smith and Hubert Walsh.

When this photograph was taken in 1956 Scarborough was still a town of character with little courts hidden away behind houses, mysterious alleys and dark passageways. We see here Lott's Yard looking towards North Street. The building on the left is the Opera House before renovation. Lott's Yard has completely vanished and the site is used as a car park.

The snow lies deep, but not crisp and even, as the milkman makes his deliveries along Atlas Place in 1956. Atlas Place ran up from St. Thomas Street between the Opera House and the Equestrian pub (the entrance is still in use today). The street was demolished in 1957 and today is a car park. The buildings on the left are the fronts of the houses in Lott's Yard, whose backs faced the Opera House. The sign advertises Boulton and Davison's Plumbers.

49

Taken in 1956, this view of Silver Street looking towards Castle Road shows the solidly built houses that look as if they would stand for ever. Sadly, in Scarborough this could never be, and since the 1970s the property in and around the area has been demolished and turned into a car park.

In November, 1956 work started on the demolition of North Terrace. We have already seen what is supposed to have been the backs of this property on another photograph.

This view taken on 21st June, 1956 shows the demolition of the water works at Cayton Bay.

Mrs. Eliza Laughton, mother of film star Charles and his two brothers Thomas and Frank, posed for this photograph in the early 1950s. She had been born Eliza Conlon and brought up at Seaham Harbour. She had run away from home and came to work in Scarborough as a barmaid in a pub run by Robert Laughton who, until then, had been a butler to a Derbyshire family. They eventually married. In time they took over the Victoria Hotel, the Pavilion in 1908, the Holbeck Hall in 1932 and the Royal in 1935. Mrs. Laughton died on 14th March, 1953.

The town had many such streets like this one made up of tidy, well-built houses. This particular view shows Regent Street, looking up from Castle Road. The year was 1957 and within three years the houses were demolished, including St. Paul's Mission which, it was said, had the largest congregation for a church its size. Flats now stand on the site.

Another view of Regent Street shows the property at its junction with William Street. The houses appear to be perfectly sound and just ideal for a family. The residents thought likewise and fought a hearty battle with the council in an effort to save their homes from demolition, but to no avail.

'Now look you here, young man' is what Ernest Bale, a West End actor, seems to be saying to young Karl, played by Sam Greetham in the Scarborough Amateur Operatic Society's 1957 production of *White Horse Inn*.

Here we see more members of the cast of *White Horse Inn*. Left to right: Sam Greetham (Karl), Mamie Benson (Kathie), F.H. Legge (Ketterl), Margaret Boag (the Mayor's secretary) and Herbert Walsh (Prof. Hinzel).

Wrea Lane, with its slaughterhouses lying opposite, was a noisy and busy thoroughfare until 1957, when these houses photographed from Sandringham Street were demolished. The houses in the distance still remain and are in use as a bed warehouse.

The empty space in the foreground is all that remains of William Street after its demolition in about 1930. This photograph was taken in 1957 and demolition is still being carried out, this time on Hepple's Grocers at the corner of Oxford Street. 'All kind of fruit in season' reads the advert on the shop front. Today the area has been tidied up somewhat and is in use as a car park.

Taken in April, 1957, Friars Entry or, as it is known today, Friarsway, was flattened by the demolition gangs as part of the council's plan to create a super modern seaside resort.

This photograph shows the backs of the properties along Friarsway prior to demolition. Today flats stand on the site.

Scarborough Corporation's Hotelescope, organized by Mr. S. Helm, Entertainments Manager, opened for two days at the Olympia Ballroom on 3rd April, 1957. Fifteen out of the nineteen stands came from Scarborough. This view shows the upstairs café; the businessmen can be seen reflected through a mirror that is painted to resemble a tropical island.

Seen here are the 3rd year juniors of Hinderwell County Modern School in 1957. Front row, left to right: 2nd Ron Kent, 5th Bobby Cheetham, 6th David Boag, 14th B. Monkman, 16th Eric Simpson and 18th Kenny Ellis. Second row: 6th Wendy Clayphan, 7th Mr. R. Pearson, 8th Miss Clare Farmborough, 9th Carolyn Streets, 10th Pat Rycroft and 12th Pat O'Neil. Third row: 5th Neil Morrison, 6th Pam Hill, 7th Crane Swiers, 8th Dave Chapman, 9th Dave Johnson, 13th John Hardman and 14th Bif Smith. Back row: 2nd Barry Louth, 3rd Brian Rhodes, 6th Mick Hartley, 7th Dave Marsh, 8th John Bell, 9th Terry Stonehouse, 11th Mick Paxton, 13th Geoff Quick, 14th Phil Ward and 15th Frank Turner.

This photograph was taken in 1957 from the window of Land's fish shop at the corner of George Street, and shows Darling's Yard off James Place. Only two of the three houses in the yard were occupied, the two residents being Mr. Thomas Birley and Mrs. Jefferson. The little lad seen playing in the yard will now be in his late 30s. The buildings seen on the left are the backs of the Wellington pub and adjacent shops. These remain, as do the outhouses, but the rest was demolished in 1960 and is now a derelict site.

Another view which is barely recognizable today. The gent standing in the middle of the road would not be doing so today with the continuous stream of traffic. The street is, of course, Northway in 1957, and the Odeon Cinema can be seen on the left. In 1960 flats were built on the open site seen fenced off and the buildings just visible on the right were demolished to make way for the Police Station that opened in 1964.

The day after this photograph was taken of Atlas Place on 15th August, 1957 the row of houses was demolished. At the far right can be seen the Equestrian pub. This remains to this day and is a pointer to those who cannot remember where Atlas Place stood.

In August, 1957 Falsgrave County Modern Girls' School won for the first time the Scarborough Schools' Swimming Championship in life saving, winning the Gibson Trophy and gaining the highest marks ever awarded to a school for diving. Front row, left to right: Sue Moody, Susan Cammish, Mary Langton, Mrs. C. Flax (coach), Frances McClure, Dorothy Leather and Florence Elliot. Back row: Sue Hilton, Janet Hewitt, Mrs. F. Fieldhouse (art mistress), Janet Coates and Jacqueline Cooke.

Hinderwell County Modern School was officially opened by the Mayor on Friday, 28th October, 1932. The architects had been Messrs. M. Clifford, Hollis and Arnott. The first headmaster and 'mistress were Mr. G. McWhan and Mrs. Lewis. Here we see a happy bunch of lads in the top playground in 1957. Front row, left to right: 2nd Eric Simpson, 3rd Frank Turner. Second row: 2nd Brian Cosham. Third row: 2nd Geoff Quick, 3rd John Hardman. Fourth row, standing: 1st Terry Stonehouse (who in 1962 won the Butler Award Competition, which was open to all secondary modern pupils). Back row: 1st Crane Swiers, 3rd Dave Smith, 5th Dave Johnson.

Friarsway in 1957, a year before demolition, captures the feel of the old town that today has all but gone. The building just showing on the right is the Oxford Hotel, which was also demolished. The council bought the land and at a cost of £21,000 erected flats on the site in 1966.

It is teatime at the *White Horse Inn* for a number of the ladies of the chorus of the Scarborough Amateur Operatic Society. A few names that are familiar are Rosamond Newham, Janet Newham, Doris Clayton, Janet Holton, Hilda Johnson, June Robson, Elizabeth Milner, Dorothy Metcalf and Violet Kemp.

Friday night may have been Amami Night, but it was also the night when all the 'way out hep cats', to use the 'in' words of the day, gathered at Roscoe Rooms for the weekly Rock'n'Roll session. Over the years Harold and Gladys France and their daughter Terry combined dancing lessons with social evenings and always managed to keep abreast of the times whether it was, old time, latin, rock or twist.

An unusual view but an interesting one as these properties are no longer standing. This photograph, dated 1957, was taken from the top window of 74 Castle Road and shows the small backyards with their coalhouses and water-closets of the houses in George Street and Regent Street.

Another view of Auborough Street taken in 1957 shows that Auborough House has been demolished and St. Mary's Parish House built on the site. The 18th century house standing to its right was pulled down two years later.

Seen dressed in the school uniform of black trousers, white shirts, yellow and green ties and sporting the school's badge with the motto 'By Wisdom and Courage' are the lads who made up the Gladstone Road County Modern Senior Boys' School Choir of 1958. They won the Eskdale Tournament of Song eight years in succession. Front row, left to right: Bob Whitehead, Keith Foster, Geoff Boyes, Mick Lauchlan, Graham Eyre, -?-, -?-. Second row: Mal Steele, -?-, -?-, Brian Snowden, -?-, -?-, John and Michael Leppington, Dave Kell, -?-, John Colishaw. Third row: -?-, Mal Stephenson, Ronnie Eade, Michael Swiers, Alan Boyer, -?-, -?-, Tony Betts, George Weller -?-, Adrian Mathews. Fourth row: Mr. Greaves (pianist), John Holborn, Ian White, -?-, -?-, Aleksander Kowalski, John Bennett, Rich Boddington, -?-, Frank Moorby, Steve Davison, Mr. Frank Spinks (deputy head and choirmaster). Back row: Ray Milburn, -?-, John Cobb, Peter Little, Chris Bagnall, Charlie White, -?-, -?-, -?-, -?-, Roy Ellicker.

Northway and Gray's corner in 1957. In 1960 flats were built on the open space and in 1990 the roundabout and obelisk were demolished to make way for a very unpopular traffic control system. The obelisk, which was erected in 1935 to act as a vent for underground toilets, was saved through the goodwill of local businessman Mr. Wilf Proudfoot, and now stands further along the street.

It was in October, 1957 that work had started on the demolition of property at the corner of Newborough and St. Thomas Street. Today a restaurant and shops occupy the site.

Another view of St. Thomas Street taken in 1957 and looking towards Newborough shows the unstoppable march of demolition. A nightclub now stands on the site.

Springfield Place in 1958 looking down past Albion Place, Castle Place and West Place. Also seen is the St. Sepulchre Street (always pronounced 'Sepulchas' by Scarborians) Primitive Methodist Chapel. On the site of this chapel stood the Church of the Holy Sepulchre built in 1267 by the Franciscians. The Primitive Methodists purchased a piece of land and their new church opened on 25th November, 1821. Adjoining land was taken over and the foundation stone for the church shown was laid on 26th October, 1865. Today all is demolished.

Ladies of the chorus of *Show Boat* on the stage of the Open Air Theatre in 1958. This show was directed by Ralph Reeder with West End players including Tudor Evans, Lorna Lee, Michael Langton and Nicholas Grimshaw. Scarborough's own players included Robert Walsh, Margaret Boag, Kenneth Snow, Mamie Benson and Leslie Mollon.

Another view of the Oxford Hotel taken from Friarsway on the day it was demolished.

Demolition started on the Oxford Hotel at the corner of Queen Street and Friarsway on 17th November, 1958. In 1890 Joseph Saynor, victualler and wine and spirit merchant, was landlord of the Oxford Hotel. The last publican was Thomas Brear in 1935. Three years later the building was being used by the Spiritualists. Today flats occupy the site.

James Beal's shop, 111 Westborough, taken in 1958. It was noted as being one of the best shops of its kind in Yorkshire. Beals closed down in the late 1980s.

In 1958 the only remaining houses in William Street were these shown on the photograph. They are still standing today although greatly altered and in use as workshops. The building with the corrugated roof was used at the time of this photograph by Swifts as a place where the refreshments were made for the workers. The sign near the car advertises Chapman's pork butchers, which was around the corner.

The caption on the back of this photograph taken in 1958 reads Springfield Place but it appears to be one of the side streets, possibly West Place, Albion Place or Castle Place. It is now demolished – whichever street it was!

Looking across the Athletic Ground to the gasometer that was demolished in the 1970s reminds one of 14th April, 1953, when workmen had been working on the 58 year old gas holder. Suddenly there had been a dull explosion and the gas envelope had surged upwards from 30ft to over 70ft. Smoke had poured out of it and nearby houses had to be evacuated. Three fire engines arrived and gas foreman Peter Hartley and two men went to the top and opened a valve which let out a gush of hot, oily air and slowly the gasometer settled.

The tranquil Italian Gardens were laid out in 1914 and are as peaceful today as yesteryear. Taken in 1959, Mr. John Morris and his son Owen relax by the lily pond.

Springtime in Scarborough. Le grand magasin Rowntree always featured style and taste in all their fashion departments. Here we see a photograph taken in 1958 of a charming model from the French Collection selected by millinery buyer, Miss I. Winter, during one of her regular spring buying trips to Paris.

In the words of Mr. Eric Mason, 'Days of wine and roses'. This photograph taken in the 1950s shows a private dinner party of Rowntree's Advisory Committee members held at the Pavilion Hotel. It was a yearly function that took place in Mrs. Eliza Laughton's sitting room on the first floor overlooking Westborough corner. Left to right: Mr. H. Gilbert, Mr A. Wallis, Mr. E. Evans, Miss N. Smith, Mr. E. Mason, Mr. D. Wilson, Miss M. Calvert

The Home and Colonial Stores, Westborough, was noted for its first-class provisions. It was demolished along with the Balmoral Hotel in 1973. Seen here are the staff in 1959. Left to right: Mr. Greetham, John Carter, Mary Dagnell, Ivy Dobson, -?-, Grace Stockdale, Netta Oliver, -?-, and Mr. Dixon. Looking at the prices one can see milk is 11d (4p) a pint, peaches 2/3d (11p) a tin and cheeses 2/- (10p) per lb.

The Spa Ballroom is shown here in 1959. The ballroom had been built in 1924 to a design by local architect Frank Tugwell. In the late 1970s an extensive refurbishment programme costing £3 million was carried out and the ballroom was greatly altered.

Quarton's Victoria Road fruit shop staff pose for this photograph in 1959. The only faces known are, left to right: 1st Gladys Dobson and 4th Mrs. Popple. Note the prices. Tomatoes 1/6d (12p) for 2lbs, bananas 1/3d (6p) a lb and dessert apples 9d (3p) a lb. Today these premises are in use as a cycle shop.

St. Thomas Street at 1.50 p.m. on a sunny day, and there is hardly any traffic! The date is 11th June, 1959 because *High Temperature* is being shown at the Opera House – admission 5/- (25p), 4/6d (22p) and 2/6d (12p). The empty space on the left is all that remains of the County Garage where today a nightclub stands.

Better days are seen here at the South Bay Pool. There is sun, crowds of happy sunseekers, and Bobby Pagan would be playing at the organ. Today the pool lies derelict and surrounded by barbed wire. This photograph was taken in 1959 and shows Pat Kidd and Barbara Dobson who have most probably spotted an eligible male. 'We're all waves and knickers' to quote Barbara, who is referring naturally to their hair and the bottoms of their swimsuits.

Picturesque little corner shops selling everything from a ball of string to a loaf of bread were a common sight when this photograph was taken of Cross Street in 1959. A year later this shop, owned by Mr. M. Worthington, and the greengrocers next door were demolished.

Today this view of Porritt's Lane running from Sandside to Quay Street is unrecognizable. In the 35 years since this photograph was taken the area has been razed to the ground.

Another view of Porritt's Lane, looking onto Sandside. The date is September, 1959, and a month later it was demolished. The entrance on the right leads into Porritt's Yard.

The Open Air Theatre at its best. What a marvellous setting for a spectacular show which appears to be the *Merry Widow* staged by the Scarborough Amateur Operatic Society.

Limekiln Hill is seen on the far right leading into Castle Road. Today it is better known as Marlborough Terrace. Its original name came from the lime kilns that were discovered in the vicinity when houses were being built. Auborough House is seen boarded up in the background, so that would date the photograph to about 1954.

This photograph taken in May, 1957 shows St. Nicholas Street without a car in sight except for the one the ladies are getting into.

The Corsair family car – selling price about £350 – had style, plenty of room and comfort.

It's all girls together on the south beach in 1959. These four beauties are members of the staff of Birdsall and Snowball's solicitors, which was situated above the bank at the corner of Huntriss Row. Their wage as shorthand typists was £3 per week. Left to right: Jennifer Knight, Barbara Dobson, Margaret Surfleet and Pauline Curtis.

The author's mother (left) and his aunt are in peaceful Sea Cliff Road in 1959. Thirty years later this road was certainly in focus, when the Holbeck Hall Hotel situated at the cliff end of it crashed into the sea.

Mr. Fred Pottage at the wheel of the Cash Supply Stores van on the pier in about 1959. The Welcome Inn Café and the Bethel Mission can be seen in the background.

St. Mary's Street is seen here in about 1959. This area was demolished around 1961 except for the three houses seen on the right and Kendall's dwellings at the top of the photograph. These had been built in 1895 by Lieut-Col. John Kendall and in time were transferred to the Trustees of the Municipal Charities.

Two
The 1960s

The 1960s was the age of the teenager. They were vibrant, heady days and young people were expressing themselves in various ways. Here we see Geoff Pearson, who so typifies the era, bopping away at the Salisbury Hotel, Huntriss Row in 1960. Shortly after this photograph was taken he joined the Sundowners – a local duo – and went on to form the Iguanas and the Mark Slade Set.

Quaint old Whitehead Hill leading down to Quay Street. Notice the Ice House on the left. This photograph was taken in 1960, and as can be seen a certain amount of demolition has already taken place. In about 1963 the whole street was demolished, except for 8 Whitehead Hill, and new houses built. The street had one public house, the Sunderland Bridge. A Mayflower car is seen parked to the left.

Imagine the smell of doughnuts and waffles drifting across the prom, and one cannot help but remember Bortoft's Waffle Shop next but one to the Corner Café. When this photograph was taken in 1960 the shop remained open till midnight. Seen here are the staff who during the winter months worked at Bortoft's Mill Street factory, making his famous, delicious pikelets. Left to right: Constance Leather, -?-, Chick, Jess and Ethel.

St. Nicholas Hotel, 1960. Plaxton's administrative staff and their wives enjoy a dinner-dance. Left to right: John Birley, Raymond Stockhill, Fred Lancaster, Dorothy Stockhill, Jennifer Birley and Betty Lancaster.

On 24th September, 1960 Scarborough won the Senior Trophy at the North Riding Schools' Swimming Gala, held at the North Bay Pool, beating Redcar 30 pts to 28 pts. Left to right: J. Lester and J. Dickinson (Boys' High School), Aleksander Kowalski (Westwood) and D. Spink (George Pindar).

In July, 1960 Westwood County Modern Senior Boys' School ran a trip to Switzerland and Italy. Here the boys and their accompanying masters are seen outside their hotel at Tesserette. The photograph was taken by one of the masters, Mr. Don Booth. Front row, left to right: John Wilson, Mal Stephenson, Bob Whitehead, Steve Davison, Blakey, -?-, Pete Liley, Mick Thompson, -?-, Mick Lauchlan, -?-, 'Wacker' Wilson, Ron Kent, -?- and Alan Pickup. Second row: Tommy Agar, Tony Brazier, -?-, M. Crosier, -?- and John Evans. Third row: -?-, -?-, John Hill, Colin Black, Francis Newham, -?-, Geoff Pearson, Paul Rippon, Geoff Boyes, -?-. Back row: Mr. John Evans, Mr. L. Rollett (Headmaster), Mr. Harry Stanworth, Dave Kell, -?-, -?-, -?- -?-, Adrian Mathews, Dennis Smith, Richard Percy and Mrs. Olive Rollett.

Another view, this time showing the front, of the Oxford Hotel in Queen Street, just before its demolition in 1958. Also seen is the headquarters of the Scarborough and District Naval Comrades Club and the R.A.O.B. (Harmony Lodge) to the hotel's right.

Rudd's fish shop, St. Thomas Street is seen here in 1960 marooned in a sea of demolition. The covered doorway leads into the Convent School. Today all is demolished and the Y.M.C.A. Theatre entrance now covers the site.

Another view of North Terrace, looking from Queen Street towards the newly built St. Mary's Parish House. All that remains today is the Scarborough Arms pub and the Granby Park Hotel, a section of which is seen on the right.

The Open Air Theatre, or 'Merrie England' as it is known to locals because of the first show staged there in 1932, looks well maintained, with holidaymakers enjoying the scenic beauty. What a difference 34 years can make to a place. Today the area lies neglected and unused, although there is a glimmer of hope on the horizon now that interest is being shown by certain parties.

On 29th September, 1960 the staff of Pacitto's Icecream Parlour and Restaurant had a day out at Blackpool. Left to right: Mrs. Appleby, Sylvia Pacitto, Mrs. Clarke, Anne Morris, Mrs. Umpleby, Penny Rowe and Pam Hodds.

Picturesque yet mysterious Quay Street in 1960 was as yet untouched by demolition. It had in the past been one of the busiest streets in town. The timbered house, 2 Quay Street, seen on the photograph probably dates back to about 1590 and is reputed to have been the home for a time of the infamous Captain Kidd. This house was restored in 1965 but all the other property, including the Ice House seen in the background, was demolished and today is a large unsightly space.

Westwood County Modern Boys' School XV rugby team, 3rd December, 1960. They had played their first match that year against Scarborough Technical College. Chris Bagnall writing in the school magazine stated, 'For the first time in the history of the school, the boys had the opportunity to play rugby football which is unique for a county modern school in the area.' Back row, left to right: A. Atkinson, J. Commins, Don Murray, G. Broadbent, B. Hopkins, Aleksander Kowalski, D. Mann and V. Wright. Front row: Gary Critchlow, D. Speight, M. Wharton, Chris Bagnall, D. Sellers, Keith Corcoran and Joe Bamfield.

At Dawnya Pickering's 21st birthday party, held at the Weydale Hotel in 1960, the girls definitely outnumbered the boys. The only faces known are, back row, left to right: 1st Colin Scott, 4th Dawnya Pickering. Front row: 3rd Robin Pickering, 4th Dorothy Laycock.

Another view of the back of Friargate taken in 1960, with Cross Street in the background. It is interesting to note that in Cross Street alone stood the Blue Bell pub, the Elephant and Castle pub, which was demolished to make way for the Market Hall, the Jolly Sailor pub, the Lamb Inn, the Red Lion pub, the Stag and Hounds pub, the Shepherds Arms pub and the Volunteer Arms pub.

This solidly-built terrace of houses connecting Barwick Street with Northway was called Unicorn Place. The date is 1961 and already the workmen have moved in to start their demolition work. The shop on the corner was, up to the end of the war, Alex Bowker's butchers. Today the Health Offices cover the site.

In 1961, to celebrate their Golden Jubilee, the famous song and laugh show, the Fol-de-Rols, returned to the Floral Hall after a three year absence. Seen at the Cricket Field are members of the cast and theatre staff who made up the Fol-de-Rols Showbiz Cricket Team. Back row, left to right: -?-, Doug Stephenson, Leslie Crowther (who was appearing in the Black and White Minstrel Show at the Futurist), Roy Sample, -?-. Front row: Chris Bryant (Stage Manager), Mr. Shields, Peter Felgate, -?-.

How views can change in a relatively short period of time is evident on this photograph taken in 1961 from the top of the Town Hall looking down onto King Street. The building centre top is the Old Savings Bank, which was taken over and used by the Housing Department. The temporary buildings are being used by the Town Hall, and the old building just seen on the right had been the Kingscliffe Holiday Camp. Today all this site is taken over by the Town Hall extensions of 1964.

On 7th October, 1961 Anne Morris married John Mitchell at St. Peter's Church. Notice the return to the more traditional style of wedding dress; in the 1950s the calf-length style had been favoured. The bridesmaids were Pam Hodds and Melanie Thornham and the best man Ian Shanks.

On 26th July, 1961 the first stones of the North Bay promenade extensions were laid. The concrete blocks were made on the site. This project marked the end of the areas tranquil beauty and of the famous Monkey Island.

A common sight in the old town in the 1960s was the boarded up windows of condemned properties. This view, taken in 1961, is of St. Mary's Street looking up from Lower Conduit Street. Off St. Mary's Street ran Barry's Passage, Adamson's Yard and Huntriss Yard. All the street was demolished in the early 1960s except for two houses. The shop facing up the street in Lower Conduit Street was the former Brass Tap public house that lost its licence in 1904.

A day trip to Whitley Bay by the pupils of Westwood County Modern School in 1961. Here we see a few of the lads. Left to right: -?-, Barry Cunnison, Richard Dixon, David Chapman, -?-, Mr. Colin Brindley (Music Master).

A lone van gingerly makes its way along the new portion of Scalby Road in the fall of 1961. In the background can be seen the Technical College that had opened the previous year. Today bungalows line this stretch of road.

Taken at the time of demolition in 1961, this photograph shows the entrance to the Savings Bank on King Street. The bank was formed in 1818 and many of the town's prominent men were connected with it. In January, 1906, in the face of competition, the managers and trustees decided to wind up the bank. On 31st July, 1906 the Scarborough Corporation purchased the premises for £1,450. The Town Hall extensions now cover the site.

Another view of the Savings Bank on King Street, which, in 1961, when this photograph was taken, was being used by the Housing Department of the Town Hall. Nesfield's Brewery is seen on the right. Nesfields lived at Auborough House in Auborough Street.

On 1st March, 1961 the final stage of laying the last connecting pipe of the southern sewerage outfall was taking place on the Foreshore. Each of these pipe sections weighed 5 tons. The total cost came to £74,830.

On Saturday, 25th November, 1961 ten employees of the Scarborough Wholesale Bakery firm of D. Wray and Sons attended a dinner-dance at the St. Nicholas Hotel to receive presentations in appreciation of their services. Back row, left to right: Mr. D. Wray, Mr. G. Whyte, Mr. B. Scaife, Mr. H. Jarvis and Mr. L. Redman. Front row: Mr. H. Needham, Mr. W. Hall (who presented the awards), Mr. E. Steele, Mr. A. Bell, Miss Ethel Stokes and Mr. J. Hargraves.

On 31st July, 1961 Scarborough Council gave the go-ahead to the Borough Engineer to demolish the Ice Factory chimney in Quay Street at a cost of £85. Workmen are seen here about to start work on the chimney which was regarded as unsafe as it leaned nine inches out of the vertical.

Northway has changed considerably since this photograph was taken in 1961. The thoroughfare had been bulldozed through Westfield Terrace, Victoria Road and half of Albion Street in 1929. The houses seen on the left are all that remain of Albion Street. Even their days were numbered, and they came down in 1962 to make way for the Police Station that opened in 1964. The shop on the left was, at the time of this photograph, Mrs. Dowson's newsagents.

A fine interior view of Gladstone Road Methodist Chapel, which was demolished in 1971.

This view of the interior of Jubilee Chapel, Aberdeen Walk was taken in 1961. In that year a 'tree of memory' was dedicated at the centenary celebrations. The painting bore the names – four hundred and sixty one in all – of all the past and present members and all the ministers of the church. Today a supermarket stands on the site.

Picturesque Paradise is seen on this photograph taken in 1961. This view, looking up from Castlegate, has completely changed today. The houses have all gone, and although new property has been built it can never recapture or compensate for the loss of the original.

St. Nicholas Street in 1961 showing the Town Hall on the right which was built in 1844 as St. Nicholas House for John Woodall, a member of a prominent banking family. The council purchased the property in 1898 and in 1903 new extensions were added. The adjoining property was demolished in 1963 to make way for further extensions. Bonnet's Chocolaterie, famous since the late 1800s for their hand-made chocolates, was one of the casualties. The horse and cart belonged to G. Newlove of 61 Tindall Street.

George Newlove's horse and cart is again seen on St. Nicholas Street, an impossibility today. The large house to the fore is the Bell Mansion, mistakenly called the Georgian House. It was built in 1708 as the summer residence of Mr. Bell, a York confectioner. The house is haunted by his daughter, Lydia, who was found murdered below the cliffs in 1804. Over the years she has been seen entering the building dressed in pink and the swishing of her dress is often heard in the corridors. Today the old building has been turned into flats.

Another view of Unicorn Place, taken from Northway in 1961 and looking towards Barwick Street. Gilbert's Café is seen to the left.

Scarborough Technical College was opened in 1960. This photograph, taken in 1962, shows a group of full-time students on the Electrical and Mechanical Pre-apprenticeship Course taking the Northern Counties Technical Examinations. Back row, left to right: Eric Wood, Brian Geraghty, Howerd Wass, Joe Readman, Jim Butchart, Mick Halliday and Malcolm Stephenson. Front row: Keith Markham, Gary Critchlow, John Moseley, Mr. Booth, Les Steele, Ronnie Eade, Richard Tankard and Colin Brett.

Holidaymakers queue for the big wheel at Butlin's Holiday Camp, Filey in 1961. Left to right: Trevor Fowler, Doreen Fowler, Christine Brown and Bunty Leather. Work had started on Butlins in 1939 but had to stop when war broke out. It was taken over by the military and Canadian and Jamaican airmen were billeted there. Butlins closed in the 1980s and for a brief period became Arntree Park.

Paradise Row was demolished in 1962. These houses had been built on the site of Mrs. Clarke's house. This lady had owned the land (Clarke's Bank) on which the present Castle Crescent now stands.

Gladstone Road Methodist Chapel was built in 1881 with extensions added in 1935. In 1963 it was decided by the Scarborough Methodist Circuit that there were too many churches in the centre of town. Its fate was sealed when the Methodist District Synod meeting in Hull agreed to its closure. On Sunday, 26th January, 1964 the closing ceremony was conducted by the Rev. E.W. Trickey. In 1971 the church was demolished.

On 27th April, 1962 the Tennyson United Football Team posed for this photograph before the game they lost 4-3 to Whitby Arcadians in the final Harbour Cup held at the Athletic ground. Back row, left to right: Arthur Bullamore, S. Smith, B. Powell, R. Smith, A. Mollon and R. Symon. Front row: J. Thompson, B. Winpenny, A. Mason, R. Drydale and John Mitchell. In 1957 this team won all the local trophies; a first in the history of football.

On 25th November, 1961 a social evening was held at the St. Nicholas Hotel for the staff of Wray's Bakers in which ten employees received long service awards. Mr. William Angus Hall, North Eastern Regional Director of British Bakeries, is seen on the left presenting the award to Mr. H. Needham, Managing Director of Wrays, to honour 26 years with the firm.

Miss Ethel (Tiny) Stokes receives her presentation watch for 25 years service to Wray's Bakery from Mr. W. Hall at the St. Nicholas Hotel on 25th November, 1961.

On 9th June, 1962 Ivor Emanuel appeared at the Futurist Theatre in *You'll be Lucky*. One high spot of the show was when he appeared on stage with the Scarborough Schoolgirls Choir. These girls had been picked at an audition the previous month from various schools. Left to right: Liz Chapman, Avril White, Shirley Schofield, Elaine Pickersgill, Wendy Cammish, Joan Codd, Ivor Emanuel, Lynne Stephenson, Patricia Hudson, Jill Scaife, Elaine Coulthard, Elsie Burton and Gillian Scullian.

Owen Morris enjoys a donkey ride on the North Sands in 1960. In the background can be seen Scalby Mills in the days before the sewerage outfall plant, amusement arcades and extension to the promenade were built.

Today this view of North Street taken from Castle Road in 1963 is unrecognizable. The second entrance with Vickerman's shop on the corner is Clarence Street. In the 1970s numbers 73-75 North Street became the 'in' place to be, when the premises opened up as the Positively Fourth Street restaurant. A vast car park now covers the site.

Christmas, 1962 at the George Hotel, Newborough. Notice the backcombed hairstyles. Left to right: Chris Benson, Alan Price, Barbara Dobson, Hazel and John Ashmore and Ray Wilson.

Seen here at the Oliver's Mount playing fields in 1962 are the Westwood County Modern School's 2nd year football team. Front row, left to right: Dave Eyre, Brian Wade, Pete Eade, David Glew and Steve Mark. Back row: John Swallow, Arthur Moss, Robert Harper, John Rowe, Geoff Smith and David Jenkinson. The school closed down in 1973 and was converted into the Stephen Joseph Theatre in the Round.

Taken from Adamson's Yard in 1963, this view shows the backs of the houses on the right hand side of St. Mary's Street. Only about two of these remain today.

Another part of Scarborough that is no more. Bradley's Corner, at the junction of Queen Street and Newborough, was demolished in 1964. Many older readers will remember Eden's Corset Warehouse; the advert can still be made out on the building and reads, 'T. Edens, Corset Warehouse, Drapery, Millinery and Corsets'. A bowling alley was built on the site, which enjoyed a brief period of popularity.

One of the top local groups was the Moonshots, which were formed in 1963. They only lasted a year before the members went their separate ways. Seen on the steps of the Olympia Ballroom are, top to bottom, Phil Peacock, Dave Rose, Pete Liley, Paddy Wilkins and Mick Rowley. Pete joined the Beat Cult and then the Mandrakes. Phil and Mick joined a York band and went to London where they recorded a disc under the name of the Shots. Phil was killed in a car crash on the Marine Drive in 1968.

Quarton's lorry on Seamer Road in 1963. Between 1959 and 1963 all the firm's vans and lorries were painted green. After that date they changed the colour to white. Of interest is the building on the left which is known today as Penquin Lodge. It is now flats but when it was built in about 1886 it was called 'Chesterfield' and was the home of the Boyes family. Whichever house they lived at included the name 'Chester'.

St. Mary's Street in 1963 still has its quaint old cottages. Seen near the gas lamp is a passageway with the name Adamson's Yard on a board above it. Today only two houses remain, including the Leeds Arms pub.

The front cover of the booklet issued to advertise the Beatles, who appeared at the Futurist Theatre on 11th December, 1963.

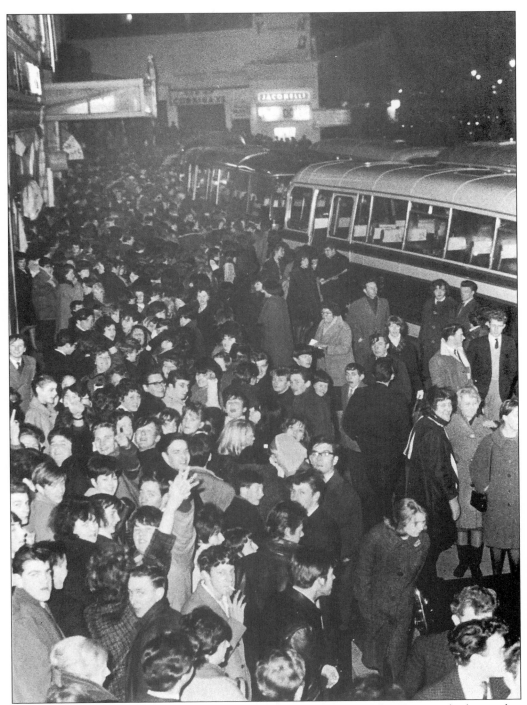

Crowds gather outside the Futurist Theatre for the arrival of the Beatles. Queuing had started at 2 a.m. for the seats, which were priced at 12/6d (62p), 10/- (50p), 7/6 (37p) and 5/- (25p). On the same bill were the Brook Brothers, Peter Jay and the Jay Walkers, the Vernon Girls and the Kestrals. The compère was Frank Berry.

Police and specials hold back the surging, screaming fans as they try to catch a glimpse of the fabulous Beatles.

Girls scream hysterically and pull their hair as the Beatles go through their numbers on stage. One lucky girl, 17 year old Judith Gullen, proudly held on to two half-smoked cigarettes that had been given to her backstage by Ringo.

A *Scarborough Evening News and Mercury* youth reporter interviews the 'Fab Four'. She was lucky; one young lady, Barbara Dobson (now Mrs. Price), was not. A friend of the Dobson family, the police inspector who had collected the Beatles from Yeadon Airport, arranged for them to call at Barbara's home at 106 Stepney Road. The Beatles had agreed and their car drove into the driveway. They knocked at the door and getting no reply drove away. Where was Barbara? She and her family were way down at the bottom of their back garden and had not heard a thing!

The Beatles make their get-away up Blands Cliff. Tempers flared on the police side as they struggled to hold back the crowds. The group's next stop was at Newcastle, but they spent the night at the Hyland's Hotel, Filey before the journey.

In January, 1964 the Y.M.C.A. Good Companions was formed by Stan Cooper, and over the years these youngsters gave professional performances wherever they were booked. Seen here are the players in the first ever pantomime, *Cinderella*, staged by the Revue Group, as they became known. Front row, left to right: Liz Chapman, Sue Pudsey, -?-, Rhys Griffiths. Back row: -?-, Alan Morgan, Elaine Clark, Jacquie Angus, Andrew Newton, Denise Hutchinson, Keith Corrie Those not on show are Liz Scott, Pete Carver, Jackie Fletcher, Jennifer Coleman and Paul Waddington.

On 1st June, 1964 the 7th Dutch Festival was opened on the Spa. The highlight of the week was the Grand Procession. Here we see what appears to be the colourful ninety-strong Horden Colliery Melody-Makers Jazz Band as they march past the now demolished Pavilion Hotel. In the crowd can be seen three familiar faces: Mr. Rooker, who worked as a carriage and wagon inspector on the railway, and Mr. and Mrs. Robinson, who lived at The Limes, Avenue Road.

A view of the interior of the Opera House taken in 1964 before it was renovated.

The Blue Stars, later known as Rikki and the Blue Stars, were formed in 1962. The members of the group were, left to right: Ken Thomas, Bob Woodyatt, Brian Thompson, Chris Bagnall and Graham Trowsdale. The band had brought the house down at an amateur band competition at the Gaiety Cinema and became an instant success in town. In time they changed their name to the Incas (who appear on another photograph).

The Floral Hall is no more, demolished in the late 1980s. A bowling centre now stands on the site. Here we see the stage hands in 1964 who made everything possible for the galaxy of stars who appeared there over the years. Front row, kneeling left to right: Colin Spivey, Shaun Brown. First row: Arthur Bowes, Alan Cowper, Len Thornton, Norman King, Harry Laycock and Bill Simmons. Back row: -?-, Terry Messenger, Nobby Clark, Arthur Watson, Doug Stephenson and Neville Barker.

The Gallon Girls go through one of their Brazilian routines at the Candlelight Club, Blands Cliff in 1963. Left to right: Pauline Dove, Pam Cook, Pat Kidd and Sue Rickartson. Note the sign at the rear, 'Bomb the Band', which must have some hidden meaning.

116

An unusual view, looking up North Street in 1965 from an upstairs window of the Y.M.C.A., shows the property on the left which was demolished in 1973 to make way for the trades entrance of a supermarket. The road leading off to the left is North Place; after passing the Scarborough and Whitby Brewery one could exit in Aberdeen Walk.

Glamorous Liz Chapman takes a break to be with her close friend Jimmy Savile in his caravan in 1965. She was, and still is, well-known throughout the town for her stage work in the Y.M.C.A. Revue Group and, later, for her singing with the professional trio Heidi's Toys.

Waves smash against the Marine Drive
sending sprays of water over 50 ft into
the air. This dramatic photograph has
captured the sheer force of the sea and
illustrates why pedestrians and cars are
urged to keep away when the sea is
rough.

It's winkle-picker shoes – note the side
laces – and drainpipe trousers – the
Beatles hairstyle goes without saying –
on Michael McKenzie (middle) and the
author (right) in 1964. Dennis Smith,
on the left, is a little more conservative,
although the pointed toe shoes are
there.

Today the Y.M.C.A. building in North Street lies empty, gutted by a fire that broke out in 1991. This photograph was taken in 1965; on the right can be seen the new coffee bar extension. The poster advertises the Beat Cult and the Incas. The Scarborough Y.M.C.A. was formed by Rev. J.A. Faithful in 1865 at 84 Westborough. It moved to Waterford Lodge, Brunswick Terrace in 1906, to 4 Pavilion Terrace in 1914, and in 1953 the North Street premises were taken over.

Wednesday, 27th October, 1965 witnessed the ceremonial opening of the Y.M.C.A. coffee bar and disco extension. The adjoining property, which had been a tobacconist's warehouse, was purchased for £6,000. Those taking part in the ceremony included, left to right, Mr. H. Edwards, Mr. R. Lyon, Mr. R. Roberts, Mr. E. Dawson, the Mayor (Councillor Whittaker), Rev. J. Keys Frazer and Mr. Bernard 'Skip' White.

Mr. Tom Colledge, who was with the Station Taxis, prepares his Humber car for a wedding in 1965.

Stan Cooper, born in Bury, became interested in the theatre when he was stationed in Japan at the end of the war. After moving from Manchester to Driffield and finally to Scarborough, he became responsible for producing the Gang Shows. He was a qualified chemist and worked at, and in the end bought, Walker's Chemist in Castle Road. He formed the Y.M.C.A. Revue Group in 1964. Stan died some years ago but is still remembered in town.

The new Y.M.C.A. coffee bar and disco gets into full swing in 1965. Admission for members was 1/9d (9p) and the Dance Club was 2/6d (12p). Some familiar faces seen on the photograph are Martin Mason, Andrew Scarborough, Colin Wood, Trevor Bell, Richard Green, John Phillips, Bob Anderson, Ross Tyson, Terry McGrath, Denise Hutchinson, Rita Waddington, Sandra Morton, Janice Griffiths and Pam Lester.

Chris Bagnall, vocalist with the Incas, shakes his maracas at the Olympia Ballroom in 1965.

Here we see the well-known faces of Elsie and Fred Robinson, who are celebrating their Golden Wedding on 17th February, 1965. Mr Robinson was one of four brothers born above the family business at 113 Falsgrave Road. He inherited his father's blacksmiths shop at the corner of Scalby Road, and iron foundry and ironmongers on Falsgrave that had been founded in 1883. He married Elsie Dodsworth in 1915 and had two children, Arnold and Margaret. He was a keen bowler and lived to be over a hundred years old.

Chirpy Les Deyes is seen in 1965 at one of the many revues he took part in. He became one of the most popular D.J.s in town and the surrounding district. He made 'pop history' (as it was called at the time) by being the first D.J. along with Dave Marshall, to appear at the Beachcomber Club, Bridlington.

This photograph of local band the Iguanas was taken in 1965, the year they were formed. Left to right: Graeme Hopwood, Brian Sharpe, John Hall, Geoff Pearson and John Pearson. They were an immediate success and supported such names as the Small Faces and Long John Baldry. In 1967 they broke up. Graeme died and John Hall sailed for South Africa. A new group was formed called the Mark Slade Set with Sandy Johnson and Calvin Turner. They were booked into the Five Acres Restaurant, East Heslerton, where they became so popular that the trade more than doubled.

In January, 1965 Stan Cooper's production of *Dick Whittington* with the cast of the Y.M. Revue Group opened at the North Street headquarters. Left to right: Sandra Symons, Rita Waddington, Keith Corrie, John Scott, Denise Hutchinson, Dennis Smith, Liz Chapman, Jacquie Angus, Geoff Ferguson, George Cree, Colin Black, Les Deyes, Chris Poulter, Penny Symons and Sue Pudsey as the cat.

John Morris prepares the bride's car at this wedding in what looks like Scalby village.

The Scarborough Millennium Festival of Norway was opened at the Spa Grand Hall by the Norwegian Ambassador on 23rd May, 1966. It was a poor week weather-wise, but heavy drizzle on the Wednesday did little to dampen the spirit of the spectators as the Grand Procession wound its way through the town. Seen here leading the sixty-four entries is Miss Millennium, Dawn Glynn, accompanied by Jimmy Savile.

Happy-go-lucky Les Deyes is the mate of the *Saucey Sal*, with Denise Hutchinson as Sarah the cook looking completely fed up with the voyage. Idle Jack played by Dennis Smith tries his best to look interested on the 'Pleasure Cruise', the theme of the sketch which went in the Y.M. pantomime *Dick Whittington* in 1965.

A group of youngsters from the Y.M.C.A. Revue Group in 1965. Familiar faces include Geoff Ferguson, Penny Symons, George Cree, Chris Poulter, Marie Thorne and John Scott.

As the Grand Procession winds its way under the Cliff Bridge lined with spectators in 1966, one's eyes move from Tesseyman's float to Gala Land, which, even though it has been demolished over 20 years, still brings back happy memories to both locals and visitors alike. Bobby Pagan is advertised on the notice board. For many years he played the organ at the South Bay Pool.

Pat Jackson in the 'Swinging City' in 1965 shows just what the modern miss was wearing in those days. Pat was a regular at the Y.M.C.A. and had, with eight other members, which included, Maureen Bailey, Graeme Cracknell and Ken Kendall, formed the 'Y' Group, whose objective was to conduct services in churches around the town. Pat is more likely to be remembered as the girl who married Harry Dunn, who became captain of Scarborough Football Club and played in all four F.A. Trophy matches at Wembley.

On 9th May, 1968 Scarborough Y.M.C.A. held its first ever Miss Y.M.C.A. competition. The contestants were, left to right: Ellen Sedman, Pam Sedman, Liz Chapman, Lesley Palmer, with Barbara Tero, Enid Spencer, Kay Smith, Jane Buchanan, Pauline Cammish, Shirley Hickman, Sandra Norton, Margaret Williamson and Linda Kelly out of view.

Ellen Sedman is crowned Miss Y.M.C.A. 1968, with Liz Chapman and Shirley Hickman joint second. The judges were Lord and Lady Downe, Mrs. E. Chapman and Mrs. A. Sibley of the Womens' Auxilliary.

At the annual dinner-dance of the Scarborough Branch of the Bakers' Union held at the Palm Court Hotel on 19th March, 1966 a presentation was made to the retired Secretary, Mr. L.C. Dove, by the present Secretary, Mr. F. Stockdale.

It's 'Hot lips Les' Deyes and 'Crazy Chris' Poulter, the Y.M.C.A.'s two swinging D.J.s, sharing a joke with Ross Tyson, the secretary and trainer of the football team in 1967.

The author in 1966 is dressed in the typical mod gear of the day: suede shoes, drainpipe trousers and leather jacket. The Beatle hairstyle was still popular but on its way out by this date. Clothes were still reasonably inexpensive in the mid-60s, a jacket costing £5, trousers 47/- (£2.35), shirts 12/6d (52p) and shoes from 25/- (£1.25) to 49/11d (£3).

Miss Carole Sharpe poses on the staircase of the Palm Court Hotel at Boyes Store's dinner-dance on 21st December, 1966. For the day, she is in the height of fashion and femininity, and shows just how nice a young person can look, which is in contrast to today's modern miss who is seen in torn jeans and men's boots. The dress would have cost anything from 21/- (£1.05) to 59/11d (£3) and the shoes about 39/11d (£2).

The Uplands, Hackness Road, the beautiful home of Miss Dorothy Robinson, racehorse owner, was sold and became the Uplands Preparatory School. It remained so until its demolition in the mid-1970s.

Photographed in November, 1966 the costume ladies of the Y.M.C.A. Revue Group, Mrs. Ann Dargue, Mrs. Margaret Jones, Mrs. Majorie Sweeting and Mrs. Edith Cooper, are seen working at full speed to get everything ready for the forthcoming Christmas pantomime. Also seen on the photograph is Mrs. 'Mick' Riches helping out.

Teenagers dance the night away at the Y.M. Disco in 1966. Les Deyes can just be seen at the turntable and a few other faces spotted in the crowd are Christine Palmer, Pauline Scott, Paul Ferguson, Barbara Tero, Sue Burns and Kenny Leith.

An extravaganza of sheer delight: yards of shimmering silks, glittering golds and silvers and dreamy pastels. Who but Rowntrees the Drapers could create such a dazzling display? In 1966 this float, entitled 'Northern Lights', gained the honour of being best in the show. The credit goes to Mr. Eric Mason and his staff, who designed and created the float with materials specially sent up from London.

The full cast of the Y.M.C.A. pantomime *Aladdin* in January, 1966. Front row, left to right: 1st Cynthia Elwick, 3rd Marilyn Robertson, 4th Denise Huchinson, 5th Penny Symons and 7th Carol Scott. Middle row: Colin Black, Dennis Smith, Rita Waddington, Vicki Ellis, Liz Chapman, Les Deyes, Chris Poulter, Adrian Kelly and Keith Corrie. Back row: 3rd Marie Thorne, 5th Marilyn Waters, 6th Pam Lester and 7th John Scott.

Vicki Ellis as the Princess and Liz Chapman as Aladdin pose at rehearsals for this well loved pantomime in 1966.

On 9th December, 1966 rehearsals took place at the Candlelight Club, Blands Cliff for a big rave night featuring the Searchers and two local bands, the Urge and A.B.C., which was to be held at the Spa. Organized by the Lion's Club, the tickets were 12/6d (62p). Here we see the models lined up. Back row, left to right: Steve Curtis, Ricky Ware, John Russell, Ian Davidson, Jimmy Mooreby, Bryan Wardman, Mick Byers and Malcolm Pobgee. Front row: Ann Lake, Pat Kidd, Pam Cooke, Pauline Dove, Ann Edwards, Susan Forcett, Jill Kirby (the last three possibly not in order) and Liz Pobgee.

Denys Grey, the resident D.J. at the Candlelight Club, plays the records for the models as they parade in the latest mod gear. Left to right: Jill Kirby, Mick Byers, Liz Pobgee, Malcolm Pobgee, Pat Kidd and Ricky Ware. The rave night at the Spa was a complete flop. Two of the Searchers failed to turn up, resulting in one Lion's member moaning, 'Scarborough is a half-crown town'.

Another view of the Y.M.C.A. in North Street, taken in 1969 and showing the property on the left which was demolished to make a new road in the early 1980s. Built to a design by J.D. Petch, the building had been opened on Wednesday, 3rd June, 1868 as a Temperance Hall. In 1892 it became the headquarters of the local Volunteer Rifles and the 2nd Battalion, Princess of Wales Own (Yorkshire Regiment). During the First World War it was used as a recruitment centre. In 1934 the Boys' Club took over and in 1953 the Y.M.C.A. joined forces and moved in. Today it lies empty, gutted by a fire which broke out in 1991.

The Beatles murals on the wall of the Y.M.C.A. coffee bar, painted by Carol Brown, look down on Jimmy Corrigan as he presents the Senior Shield to the Arabs player Phil Cook (right) and the Junior Cup to the Barrons player Derek Weller at a presentation ceremony held in January, 1967.

Susan Richards and a number of her ballet pupils are seen here in 1967 in the now demolished Christ Church. In addition to teaching her own pupils she also helped choreograph many of the shows at the Floral Hall. Left to right: Denise Mann, Mary Jane Watkinson, Edna Davis, -?-, Patricia Dalton and Susan Richards.

In about 1964 the local band Rikki and the Blue Stars changed their name to the Incas. Left to right: Ken Thomas, Brian Thompson, Bob Woodyatt, Chris Bagnall and Pete Hargreaves. During a summer season at Hornsea they met Mike Berry, an agent from London. The result was that in October, 1965 they travelled to London and recorded a disc written for them by the Small Faces entitled, 'One Night Stand'. They returned to Scarborough and the group disbanded. Chris died in about 1986 and Brian in 1993. Bob is the only one still playing. He joined up with Ian Fletcher and the two of them are popular around the clubs.

Boyes Staff dinner-dance at the Palm Court Hotel on 21st December, 1966 Mrs. Beryl Cousins can be seen (left) as the Sheik of Araby and John Boag as one of the harem girls. In the background are Richard Dolan, Geoff Boyes, Carol Pipes and Richard Percy.

137

By 1967, when this photograph was taken, the Y.M.C.A. Revue Group was 3 years old and had become very popular. Here we see the principals of *Mother Goose* on stage at St. Mary's Parish House. Back row, left to right: Keith Corrie, Shirley Hickman, Vicki Ellis, Dennis Smith, Liz Chapman, Denise Hutchinson, Sheila Fairlie and Colin Black. Front row: Les Deyes, Marie Thorne, Ron Smithson, Joan Rowley and Chris Poulter.

The Honory Choreographers, Barbara and Mamie Benson, take the dancers through their paces for the *Quaker Girl* staged in 1967. On the photograph are Jill Blackburn, Josephine Carter, Susan Cook, Denise Gretton, Susan Harrop, Christine Scott and Sandra Smith, with Lynda Davison and Linda Cowton as the principal dancers.

Mamie Benson as the Grand Duchess Anastasia in the 1967 production of the *Student Prince*. Mamie first danced at 13 years of age, when she was a soubrette in a Morecambe concert party. In the 1920s she played principal boys and understudied Florrie Ford. During the war she toured Europe with E.N.S.A., and on her return to Scarborough formed her own dancing academy. Mamie is now nearly 90 years of age but is still active in raising money through her shows for charity. Over the years she must have raised well in excess of £70,000 and if anyone deserves an honour then this lady must rank at the top.

Jimmy Savile with his mother, who lived at Wessex Court on the South Cliff, stands talking to youngsters in the Station forecourt before the sponsored walk to Filey on 7th January, 1968.

139

On 7th January, 1968, in cold drizzle, fifty young people took part in a sponsored walk to Filey and back to raise funds for the Y.M.C.A. Jimmy Savile led off the walkers. Eight young men led by Jimmy Corrigan decided to run there and back. The winner was Ian Taylor followed closely by Mr. Corrigan, George Crosier and David Horne. Also seen on the photograph is Ross Tyson.

A happy gathering at Wallis's Holiday Camp in 1968. They are the staff and families of Boyes Store. Some known faces are Fred and Dolly Pottage, Frances and James Percy, Janet and Carol Pipes, and Ray and Mrs. Faulkner.

'Hot Lips Les' Deyes and 'Crazy Chris' Poulter, the two resident Y.M. disc jockeys, join forces with Jimmy Savile to spin records in the Coffee Bar and Disco in 1968. Les went on to be the resident D.J. at the Whitehall Shipyard Club in Whitby and later the Scarborough Candlelight Club. Chris became resident D.J. at Wallis's Holiday Camp and then moved to York.

It looked the typical corner shop except for one difference: next to the provisions was a row of beer pumps and two bar stools. This could only be the Denmark Arms in St. Mary's Walk, which was built in 1850. When this photograph was taken in 1969 it was said to be one of the smallest pubs in Britain. It was originally owned by Scarborough and Whitby Breweries but was taken over by Camerons. John Firth was the landlord when the pub closed down in September, 1972. Today it is a private house.

Victoria Road is seen here at the end of the decade, before the road was widened to allow two-way traffic. The block of houses on the right was demolished in the early 1980s and a car park built.

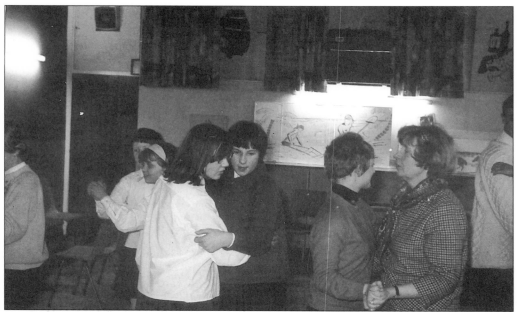

It's left-foot-forward, one-two-three, one-two-three, at the Y.M.C.A. in 1967 as members go in for a little ballroom dancing. Shirley Hickman, 'Mick' Riches, Keith Corrie and Denise Huchinson appear to be enjoying themselves.

Even as late as the 1960s Scarborough could boast of having a fair number of quaint and interesting little yards tucked away behind old cottages. Here we see Porritt's Yard, which stood off Sandside. It would appear that someone still lives there as the coal bunker is full of coal.

Taxi driver John Morris washes his Humber car in the town's first car wash in Brook Street in 1969.

Meg Somers, who died in 1993, was a true 'bottom ender' having been born and bred in what was known as the East Ward. She was well-known throughout that area for her neighbourly ways and the spicey and interesting tales she told of the residents of that part of town. Although the author knows many a tale that she told him, most of them are unprintable.

Thirty years on, Pete Liley, ex Moonshot, Beat Cult and Mandrake guitarist, is still belting out the old numbers around the town's pubs and clubs in the Mick Wheeler Band.

'When Irish Eyes Are Smiling' is the name of the sketch from the Y.M.C.A. revue, *This is Your Life*, staged at the Floral Hall on 27th May, 1968. It was an outstanding success for the fifty members of the cast. Seen on this photograph are Ron Austwick, Michael Carr, Tina Bradley, Jane Buchannan, Keith Corrie, Liz Chapman, Joyce Dykes, Ian Fletcher, Stephen Foxton, Hazel Mansfield, Dave McGregor and Ray Shillito.

Mr. Herbert Rewcroft, lumper for the Filey United Fish Company, poses with the shark that was landed at Scarborough harbour in 1969.

Miss Y.M.C.A. 1969, Linda Cowton, presents a cup to the six-a-side football team at Northstead playing fields. Front row, left to right: Ronnie Lamb, Billy Blades. Back row: -?-, Dennis Anderson, Robert Chamberlain, Ray Welford.

The versatility of the Gallon Girls is evident on these two photographs taken at Emma's Nightclub in 1967. Whether it be the Charleston with Pam Cooke and Pat Kidd, or the Hippy Shake with Pat Kidd, Pam Cooke, Liz Pobgee and Pauline Dove, the audience sit spell-bound while Geoff Laycock and his Band swing away in the background.

On Wednesday, 8th May, 1968 the main hall of the Y.M.C.A. North Street was full for the annual presentation of awards. Present were Lord and Lady Downe, Rev. J. Keys Frazer and other guests. Here we see Derek Oldroyd, footballer of the year, receiving his trophy from Lord Downe.

Two players with the Saints four-a-side football team, Terry Dobson (left) and Tony Mancrief, receive their prizes from Lord Downe.

Gerry Baldwin (2nd left) looks pleased with himself as he receives his award for his skills in playing with the Y.M. Hornets.

In August, 1968, at a ceremony held in the gym of the Y.M.C.A. in North Street, the chairman of the Members' Committee, Chris Poulter, presented a scroll and a cigarette case to Mr. Bernard White, the General Secretary of the club. After 6 years he was leaving with his family to take up a post in Nairobi, Kenya, where he was to teach and train national secretaries.

Local group the Mandrakes was formed in 1966 and lasted until 1971. Left to right: Mick Cook, Pete Liley, Allen Palmer, Rich Hodgson and Mick Stephenson. In 1969 Palmer joined Alan Bown, changed his name to Robert Palmer, and is now internationally known. The Mandrakes were one of the most popular bands in town and also in Europe when they toured Denmark in 1969.

Clarabelle the cow obviously does not want to go to the market despite the combined efforts of Widow Wallop (Dennis Smith) and Jack (Liz Chapman). A scene such as this could only come from Stan Cooper's 1969 pantomime *Jack and the Beanstalk*.

Photographs such as this one showing the backs of houses in St. Thomas Walk and Atlas Place (on the left) from the yard of Premier Engineering in St. Thomas Street do not have a lot of detail but they are so interesting because they show areas of the town that would never be seen by the public at large simply because they were out of sight.

On Saturday, 15th February, 1968 three commemorative stones were laid in the extension to Wreyfield Drive Methodist Church by Mrs. May Wood on behalf of Scarborough Methodist Circuit, Mr. Richard Trott (Wreyfield Drive Society) and Mr. Doug Stephenson (Gladstone Road Society). Also in attendance were Rev. J.E. Christian, Rev. T. Johnson and Miss Ida Slarke.

Liz Chapman joined with John Curtis and Robin Hanlon to become the vocal harmony trio, Heidi's Toys. They performed for the first time professionally on 23rd March, 1969 with Graham Hopwood in the place of Robin at Carlin Howe, near Loftus. The trio became popular on the north east coast circuit and had engagements on cruise ships sailing to the Canary Islands.

Mother Goose at St. Mary's Parish House in the late 1960s. Two of the principals, Vicki Ellis and Denise Hutchinson, go over their lines. In the chorus line can be seen, left to right: 1st Marilyn Robertson, 3rd Joyce Dykes, 5th Shaun Wilson, 9th Marilyn Waters and 10th Stephen Foxton.

What can one say about this view of the Suncourt on the Spa? The picture says it all. Sun, sea and the melodious sound of the Spa Orchestra playing to the ideal holidaymaker, which Scarborough once used to favour so much but which today is in the minority, having been replaced by young people who seek noise, clubs and pubs.

In a setting of peaceful beauty created by the light from hundreds of candles, miniature bulbs and an illuminated Christmas tree, carols were sung by the Central Hall Choir in Queen Street Chapel on Boxing Day, 1969. The programme had been directed and arranged by Mr. Leslie Sturdy and Rev. John Dover, M.A.

The Butter Cross at the corner of Pump Hill, or to give it its correct name West Sandgate, is believed to date back to 1670, when it stood in Carr Street (now Cross Street). It was erected in Lower Conduit Street in the 19th century. The building on the right was built in the 1960s on the site of the Brass Tap pub. The Leeds Hotel on the left is considered to be the most attractive pub in town. It dates from 1693 but was greatly renovated in 1900 by Frank Tugwell.

Dog and Duck Lane leading from Sandside to Quay Street has one of the few remaining old properties in the old town. The building on the right is the Lancaster Inn, which dates back to about 1870. The old timbered building, also part of the Lancaster Inn, was originally the Dog and Duck pub; it was incorporated into the Lancaster during the latter half of the 19th century.

It's Beat Nite at the Y.M.C.A. in the late '60s. The faces are familiar but the names have gone.

It is as though Susan Richard's School of Ballet are saying, 'welcome to the 1970s' at the show *Living it Up* at the Floral Hall. Back row, left to right: Melanie Agar, Sarah Sutcliffe, Denise Mann, -?-, Elaine Arber, Susan Showers, Wendy Stephenson, Susan Barber and Beverly Clarke. Two in the middle: Julie Dargue and Katrina Flynn. Bottom row: Deborah Pobgee, Paul Cooper, Alison Amos, Annette Hargrave, Nicholas Tapsell, Shan McIndoe, Michelle Robinson, Sid Cooper and Louise McKenzie.

Acknowledgements

I am indebted to Yorkshire Regional Newspapers and to Mr. Richard Welford Smith, LPIPP, LMPA for their help, and to the following for allowing me access to their photographic collections:

Mrs. Lynne Appleby, Mrs. Edie Arnold, Miss Mamie Benson, Mr. Bryan Berryman (Ref. Librarian), Miss Liz Chapman, Mr. Keith Corrie, Mr. Peter Eade, Mr. George Edmonds, Mrs. Georgie England, Miss Clare Farmborough, Mrs. Pat Fleming, Miss Pat Kidd, Mr. Aleksander Kowalski, Mrs. Betty Lancaster, Mr. Peter Liley, Mr. Eric Mason, Mr. Edward Midgley, Mrs. Anne Mitchell, Mr. John Mitchell, Mrs. F. Morris, Office Equipment Bureau, Mrs. Netta Oliver, Mr. Geoffrey Pearson, Mr. Chris Poulter, Mrs. Barbara Price, Mr. Gordon Rewcroft, Miss Susan Richards, Mrs. Betty Ross, Mr. and Mrs. E. Sedman, Mr. Doug Stephenson, Mrs. Jacquie Stephenson, Mr. Malcolm Stephenson, Mrs. Margaret Stephenson, Mr. David Stokes, Mrs. Ann Webster, Mr. Chris Wilby (Scarborough Y.M.C.A. Sec.) and Mr. Bob Woodyatt. And to my mother and father.